Thinking In Constellations

Thinking In Constellations:

On Writing, Memory, and the Art of Time

By Elidio La Torre Lagares

Thinking in Constellations:
On Writing, Memory, and the Art of Time

This book is a work of nonfiction. All reflections, narratives, and exercises are presented for literary, educational, and reflective purposes. The author does not offer medical, psychological, or therapeutic advice. Readers should consult qualified professionals regarding any health-related concerns.

Some names, identifying details, and situations have been altered or generalized in the interest of privacy.

First edition, 2026

ISBN: 979-8-90452-947-5
Printed in the United States of America

TRON BOOKS
P.O. Box 79509
Carolina, PR 00984-9509

My body is a record of my life.
—Annie Ernaux

Contents

Thinking In Constellations

> Not everything unwritten is lost.
> Some things wait for the right voice.

This book begins with a quiet but urgent proposition: that writing is not merely an artistic act, nor simply a therapeutic one, but a cognitive practice—a way of keeping the mind awake to itself across time. In later life, when memory begins to shift its habits and attention adopts a different rhythm, writing becomes more than expression. It becomes a form of maintenance. A form of care.

As we age, the mind does not empty. It reorganizes. What weakens is not intelligence but speed; what intensifies is density. Memory grows less linear and more layered. We forget names even as we remember atmospheres. We lose chronology but gain pattern. This transformation is often narrated as decline, yet psychological research and lived experience suggest another reading: that later cognition is not diminished, but reoriented.

Thinking In Constellations was written for those who sense this reorientation and wish to inhabit it consciously. It is intended for people who want to exercise their cognitive and mnemonic capacities not through abstraction or drills, but through language, attention, and narrative reflection. Writing, in this context, is not about productivity or literary ambition. It is about keeping the mind in motion by giving it meaningful work to do.

Over the past several decades, research in psychology and health has confirmed what poets and elders have long known: that sustained, reflective writing produces measurable effects on well-being. James W. Pennebaker's work on expressive writing demonstrates that regularly putting lived experience into words helps regulate stress, improves emotional processing, and correlates with better physical and mental health outcomes. Writing does not heal by erasing pain, but by organizing experience, allowing the mind to metabolize what would otherwise remain lodged in the body as tension, inhibition, or fatigue.

What matters most in these studies is not literary skill. It is engagement. The mind benefits when it is invited to make meaning—when it is asked to connect events, sensations, and emotions into a form that can be revisited, revised, and held. Writing exercises the same cognitive faculties that aging threatens to isolate: attention, recall, sequencing, metaphor, judgment, and emotional differentiation.

But *Thinking In Constellations* does not approach writing as a clinical intervention. It does not promise cure, prevention, or optimization. Instead, it understands writing as a narrative practice, one that supports health indirectly by sustaining coherence, agency, and relational identity.

Narrative therapy has shown that identity is not a fixed essence but an ongoing composition shaped by the stories we tell about ourselves and the stories that have been told to us. As Sonia Abels and others in narrative traditions argue, when stories remain unexamined, they harden into fate; when they are re-entered with curiosity, they regain movement. Writing allows us to revise—not the facts of our lives, but the meanings we have assigned to them.

This matters deeply in later life. Aging introduces losses that are not only physical but narrative: the loss of roles, of futures once imagined, of versions of the self that quietly recede. When these changes are not narratively integrated, they often appear as confusion, withdrawal, or despair. Writing offers a way to re-situate experience, to say: this, too, belongs to my story.

At the same time, creative-writing psychology reminds us that imagination does not disappear with age; it changes its task. As Scott Barry Kaufman and James C. Kaufman observe, creativity in later life often becomes less about novelty and more about synthesis. The mind shifts from generating endless possibilities to integrating what has already been lived. This integrative creativity is precisely what reflective writing cultivates.

The exercises in this book are designed with this in mind. They do not demand speed or volume. They favor slowness, return, repetition. They ask the writer to revisit memory from different angles, to translate sensation into metaphor, to approach experience through the body as well as through thought. Each exercise recruits multiple cognitive systems at once, encouraging flexibility rather than mastery.

Yet this book is not only about keeping the brain alert. It is also about assuming one's life.

At a certain point, experience asks to be looked at—not nostalgically, not defensively, but honestly. We begin to feel the weight of what has been lived: the relationships that shaped us, the decisions that altered our direction, the losses that reorganized our priorities. Writing becomes a space where these elements can coexist without being forced into resolution.

Spiritual writing traditions have long understood this function. Janet Conner's work on sacred journaling emphasizes that writing is not always a means of expression but a form of listening—an attunement to what life has already inscribed within us. In this sense, writing does not impose meaning; it receives it.

Thinking In Constellations adopts this posture. It treats experience not as raw material to be exploited, but as a record to be honored. The goal is not to produce a definitive account of one's life, but to enter into dialogue with it—to recognize patterns, tensions, continuities, and silences.

This dialogue is never solitary.

Every life is lived in relation. Our memories are braided with those of others: parents, teachers, lovers, children, friends, strangers who crossed our path briefly but decisively. When we write our lives, we inevitably write about others—and in doing so, we discover that the self is not a singular voice but a chorus.

This recognition gives the book its title. *Thinking In Constellations* is not a memoir in the traditional sense. It is an invitation to write oneself into a collective narrative, to acknowledge that personal memory is also cultural memory, relational memory, inherited memory. Writing becomes a gesture of belonging rather than self-assertion.

The chapters of this book do not follow a linear curriculum. They move instead through the body, memory, grief, time, plurality, and continuity—because this is how meaning actually emerges in later life. The structure mirrors cognition itself: associative, recursive, attentive to return.

You will find no promise of mastery here. Only practice.

This book does not ask you to become younger, sharper, or more efficient. It asks you to become more present to what has already been lived—and to keep that presence active through language. Writing, in this sense, is not an escape from aging. It is a way of inhabiting it with intelligence, dignity, and generosity.

If you engage these pages with patience, curiosity, and care, writing may become what it has always been at its deepest function: a way of staying awake to one's own life—and of leaving behind a trace that others may one day recognize as theirs.

This is not a book about the isolated self.
It is a book about relation.

It is not a book about endings.
It is a book about continuation.

Welcome to *Thinking In Constellations: Writing, Memory, and the Art of Time*.

Warm-Up Stage: Claiming a Place to Speak

You may write tenderly, cautiously, humorously, or sparsely.

There is no obligation to reassure or instruct.

You are not writing to be remembered. You are writing to be felt.

Before memory is examined, before grief is named, before the plural voice emerges, the writer must first occupy a position. This is the place where all your stories are emitted as energy, because energy is information.

The following exercises do not ask for skill or explanation. They ask for presence. They establish a ground from which writing can occur.

This warm-up is about locating the self in language—not as identity, but as existence.

Exercise I: Letter to the Unborn Reader

To situate you in relation to time and to acknowledge that every act of writing is addressed, even when the addressee is unknown.

Prompt:
Write a short letter to someone who may encounter your words fifty years from now.

Do not explain who you are. Do not summarize your life. Instead, let your tone, your choice of details, and your silences reveal you.

Ask yourself:

- What would you want this reader to *feel* in your presence?
- What trace of your way of being would you want to remain?

Exercise II: Inventory of Unwritten Things

To acknowledge the interior archive—the experiences that have existed without language—and to affirm that what has not yet been written still belongs to the self.

Prompt:
Make a list of things you have carried but never written:

- stories,
- images,
- sensations,

- moments without explanation,
- memories without a place to land.

Do not judge the list. Do not order it.Choose one item.

Describe it in two or three short paragraphs, as if it were a living being still waiting for its moment to arrive. Do not explain its meaning. Attend to its presence.

Ask yourself:

- Where has it been living?
- What has it been waiting for?
- What happens now that it has been seen?

Exercise III: The Door You Haven't Opened Yet

Establish your awareness of threshold—of choice, hesitation, and latent possibility. Describe a door you have not yet opened. It may be literal or metaphorical.

Attend carefully to:

- the door itself,
- what lies behind it (imagined or known),
- what has kept you from crossing.

Then write one paragraph answering this question: *What would change—not immediately, but eventually—if you opened it?*

Do not resolve the crossing.

The exercise ends at the threshold.

Closing Note for the Warm-Up Stage

These exercises do not seek confession or explanation. They establish stance. By completing them, the writer has done something essential: they have claimed a position in time, memory, and language.

From here, writing can begin—not as recollection, but as presence.

You are not required to enter. You are required only to stand before what exists.

Growing Still

The day I sat down to write this book was not a day at all, but a realization—quiet, precise, irreversible. It arrived not with the gray hair or the mirror, but with the understanding that time had become visible inside me: the body speaking the truth the mind had long postponed. I discovered then what aging really is—not a decline, but a change of narrative tense. Life shifts from "I will have done" to the simple "I am."

I began writing this book not to teach, but to remember—and perhaps to remember differently.

For years, as a teacher of writing, I asked my students to turn their lives into stories. I urged them to find meaning in the ordinary, structure in the passing hour, metaphors in the daily act of being alive. When I finally sat to write *Thinking in Constellations*, I realized that I was asking the same of myself: to find the story in aging, to write not from nostalgia but from continuity.

This book is not a memoir, though it begins in memory. It is not a manual, though it invites you to write. It is a dialogue—between the self and its many versions, between the writer and the reader, between solitude and community. Its chapters follow a path as old as time itself: from awareness, to presence, to renewal, to embodiment, to release, to belonging. Each offers not conclusions but beginnings, not lessons but invitations.

This is a book for those who have reached a point in life where the future no longer looks like a straight road, but like a vast horizon—wide, uncertain, luminous. I wrote it for those who have lived enough to know that stories are not possessions but gifts, that writing is not a record of permanence but a gesture of offering.

The exercises at the end of each chapter are simple doors. They do not require technique or ambition, only sincerity. They are meant to awaken what remains vital within us: curiosity, tenderness, the quiet astonishment of still being here. After all, *Thinking in Constellations* is not mine. It belongs to everyone who reads it, everyone who writes alongside it, everyone who has ever looked back and whispered: So this is what it means to have lived.

We are, each of us, made of time, body, and story. But when we write—truly write—we become more than ourselves. We become part of the great human chorus that continues speaking long after the voice is gone.

This, then, is not a book about growing old. It is a book about growing still—about listening to the echo of life as it continues, beautifully, through us all.

The Day I Got Old

The day I got old was not marked by wrinkles or fatigue, nor by the slow betrayal of strength I had always assumed would announce it. It arrived quietly, disguised as information. I learned that my coronary arteries were stiffened, narrowed, clogged almost to the point of collapse. Nearly one hundred percent. The numbers were precise. Their meaning was not.

I had always exercised. I still do. Four days a week, sometimes more. My doctor had recommended a minimum of one hundred and fifty minutes of cardiovascular activity per week, and I exceeded it easily—cycling, spinning, moving my body as if movement itself were a form of reassurance. I had no symptoms. No shortness of breath. No pain radiating into the arm. No warning signs that popular narratives teach us to expect. I had even lost forty-five pounds in the months before the diagnosis, convinced—like so many—that effort was a kind of immunity.

And yet, there it was. A body carrying a history it had never been spoken aloud.

Today, as I write these words, I still do not know what lies ahead. Perhaps by the end of this book I will know more. Perhaps I will not. What I do know is simpler and more difficult to ignore: time lived is time precious. Whatever comes next does not erase what has already been. I know the past. I have inhabited it.

"We are made of stories," Herta Müller once wrote. I later heard Toni Morrison echo that conviction in an interview, as if the idea had been circulating long before either of them gave it language. Eduardo Galeano, too, believed that we are not made of atoms and space, but of the past—of memory sedimented into narrative. The past is not inert. It is active. It is the tale we tell ourselves in order to remain intelligible.

Time, for me, has always been a structure—a way of measuring the length of the road we travel. But as we move along that road, things happen. And things are matter. Not always physical, not always visible, but often more decisive than either. Call them intangible. Call them spiritual. Call them metaphysical, if you like. I will call them memories.

The Italian poet Cesare Pavese was convinced that we do not remember days, but moments. He was right. No one recalls an entire year intact. We remember instants that have condensed meaning: a voice on the phone, a look exchanged across a room, the particular weight of a sentence that arrived at the wrong—or perfect—time. Memory is not chronological; it is selective, but not arbitrarily so. It chooses what altered us.

My grandmother, who raised me and shaped much of who I became, used to say that life begins by going uphill, reaches a peak, and then, inevitably, begins its descent. She did not say this bitterly. It was simply how things were. Today, I cannot help hearing in her metaphor the structure of narrative itself: an opening, a rising tension, a limit situation, and then a slow movement toward resolution. A formula as old as the Greek philosopher Aristotle.

The Aristotelian reference does not come freely, of course. Philosophy never does. Philosophy is not a luxury reserved for classrooms or treatises. It is an activity we perform simply by living. It is the work of asking why this mattered, why that choice was made, why one path was taken over another. Even dismissing philosophy as useless is already a philosophical act—one that assumes a certain idea of value, purpose, and relevance.

As we age, we become philosophers almost without realizing it. We look back, not out of nostalgia, but out of necessity. We want to discern the structures that shaped our ways of seeing, valuing, deciding. Whether those structures served us well or poorly is not the central question. What matters is the distillation: the residue of experience, the lessons learned without instruction, the stories that brought us here—right here, at this moment of looking back and forward at once.

Illness, especially when it arrives without warning, sharpens this retrospective impulse. It forces a reckoning with time not as abstraction, but as condition. Suddenly, the future is no longer an open expanse; it is a question. But the past, paradoxically, becomes more solid. It gains weight. It asserts itself.

This is what I mean when I say that the day I got old was not the day my body weakened, but the day my time became visible. Aging, in this sense, is not simply the accumulation of years, but the moment when one's narrative coherence comes into focus. You realize that your life has already said something, whether you intended it to or not.

And that realization carries responsibility.

We matter. Not in the inflated sense of achievement or recognition, but in the quieter sense of continuity.

We matter because we make the past possible. Because our sons and daughters, our students, our grandchildren—and even strangers we will never meet—walk the same road at a considerable distance behind us. They will find traces. They will find stories. They will recognize themselves in fragments of what we have lived.

Just as we once recognized ourselves in the lives of those who came before us.

You are not here to recover youth, nor to summarize a life.

You came here to recognize the intelligence of having lived — and to place that intelligence into a language of your own.

The act of telling our stories is not a sign of vanity, but of generosity. It is a way of saying: you are not alone in this confusion, this fear, this effort to make sense of a life that rarely unfolds as planned.

Writing, at this stage, is less about invention than about transmission.

Less about proving something new than about offering what has already been learned at the cost of living.

I do not know what the rest of my road will look like. But I know the shape of the path behind me.

And I know that paths exist not only to be walked, but to be followed.

That knowledge, more than any diagnosis, is what marks the beginning of old age—not as decline, but as awareness.

Exercises Chapter 1

1. The Exact Moment

Return to the precise instant when you first sensed that time had shifted for you—not intellectually, but bodily. The moment when youth quietly loosened its hold.

Write a paragraph or short scene using **only sensory detail**:

- sound
- texture
- light
- breath
- temperature
- weight

Do not use abstract words such as *age*, *old*, *time*, *future*, or *past*.
Let the body speak before the mind interprets.

Purpose:
To locate aging not as an idea, but as an event—an experience registered first by sensation, not concept.

2. The Mirror Dialogue

Exercise:
Stand before a mirror, or imagine one.

Write a brief dialogue between your present self and the younger self reflected there.
Each voice may ask **only one question**:

- The younger self asks: *What did I forget?*
- The older self asks: *What have you learned?*

Write their answers without explanation or defense.
Let the exchange remain incomplete.

Purpose:
To integrate the self who lived with the self who remembers—without hierarchy, nostalgia, or judgment.

3. The Mountain of Life

Your grandmother described life as a climb, a peak, and a descent.

Imagine—or sketch—your own mountain:

- label its inclines, plateaus, descents,
- mark places of rest, loss, silence, acceleration.

Do not aim for completeness. Let the omissions speak.

Then write a short piece titled **"The View from Here."**

Transform autobiography into landscape, allowing structure—not chronology—to shape memory.

4. The Story That Made Me

Choose one story from your past that still exerts quiet authority over who you are:

- a sentence someone once said,
- an encounter that altered your direction,
- a moment of courage, shame, or recognition.

Rewrite this event **as if told by someone who loves you**, someone who is trying to understand you rather than judge you.

Change the point of view.
Keep the facts.
Alter the tone.

Introduce compassion and craft into memory—see yourself not as subject, but as character.

5. Philosophical Inventory

Make a list of **five beliefs** you once held as truths but no longer do.

For each, write one sentence beginning with:

I used to think… but now I know…

Then add **one belief you still hold without question**—and do not explain why.

6. The Narrative of the Arteries

In this chapter, aging begins not with appearance, but with the discovery of blocked arteries.

Invent your own metaphor for how **time moves through your body now**.

Is it:

- blood,
- breath,
- current,
- sediment,
- thread,
- tide?

Describe how this inner movement flows, slows, pauses, or redirects—and what it carries with it.

End with one sentence beginning:

This is what time feels like inside me.

Merge the physical and the metaphysical—to write aging as circulation rather than decline, as story rather than diagnosis.

What Day Is Today?

When I was a child, my mother—who was a schoolteacher her entire life—kept books everywhere. They were not arranged ceremoniously on shelves; they lived among us. They lay open on tables, rested on chairs, migrated from room to room. Reading, for her, was not an activity but an atmosphere.

Among those books, I remember a worn copy of *Winnie-the-Pooh* by A. A. Milne—the early stories, before Pooh became a global icon. In one of those quiet, luminous scenes, Piglet—Pooh's companion, his trembling double, his emotional echo—asks a question that seems almost absurd in its simplicity:

"What day is it?"

Pooh, gentle and unhurried, replies:
"Today."

Piglet pauses, then says:
"My favorite day."

Nothing more needs to be added.

No calendar. No schedule. No nostalgia or anticipation. The scene proposes something radical: that presence outweighs measurement, that existence matters more than timekeeping. *Today* is not a point on a line but a fullness. It is enough.

The present, after all, is never isolated. It carries with it everything we have lived, everything that has shaped us. *Today* is a continuation, not an interruption. It gathers what came before and offers it back to us, quietly.

In another book my mother placed in our hands, I encountered *The Little Prince* by Antoine de Saint-Exupéry. Many of you will remember it. At its center is a journey—not only across planets, but across ways of understanding the world.

Before arriving on Earth, the Little Prince travels from asteroid to asteroid, encountering figures that belong unmistakably to the adult world: the king obsessed with authority, the vain man hungry for admiration, the drunkard trapped in shame, the businessman counting stars he cannot use, the lamplighter bound to routine, the geographer who never leaves his desk. Each inhabits a world governed by abstraction—power, prestige, accumulation—things that can be quantified but not truly lived.

When the Prince finally reaches Earth, he wanders through the desert. He meets a snake. Then, unexpectedly, he discovers a garden full of roses.

This devastates him.

Memory is not an archive.
It is a material — alive, unstable, generous.

And so are you.

On his small asteroid, he had believed his rose to be unique—the only one of her kind. Now he stands before hundreds, indistinguishable from one another. His grief is not botanical; it is existential. He feels deceived. He feels ordinary. He doubts the meaning of what he has loved.

It is precisely then that he meets the Fox.

The Fox does not appear as a threat, but as a presence. Shy. Attentive. A creature who understands solitude. When the Prince asks him to play, the Fox replies:

“I cannot play with you. I am not tamed.”

The word *tamed* becomes the axis of their encounter. The Fox explains that to tame someone is to establish ties—to create a relationship in which two beings become unique to one another. Love, the Prince learns, is not a property of objects. It is a practice. A duration. A devotion.

Later, the Fox offers his secret:

“It is only with the heart that one can see rightly; what is essential is invisible to the eye.”

When the Prince returns to the rose garden, nothing has changed—except him. The roses are still beautiful, still abundant. But they are empty of relationship. His rose, back on his asteroid, is unique not because she is rare, but because of the time he has given her. Watering. Protecting. Listening. Waiting.

Time, he realizes, is what gives meaning.

You might say: this is a children's story. And yes, it is. But that does not mean it is childish?

The psychologist Carl Jung believed that the child and the elder are not opposites, but mirrors. Both stand close to mystery. Both exist near the edges of language. The child has not yet mastered it; the elder begins, slowly, to release it. Between them lies the long corridor of adulthood—duty, productivity, explanation.

Aging, then, is not simply decline. It is a return—this time with memory, depth, and discernment. If childhood is imagination without experience, aging can become imagination *informed* by experience.

We are often told that growing older means losing things: speed, certainty, roles. But it also means gaining something rarer: the ability to see without urgency, to value without possession, to speak without proving.

> **Some days linger. They resist closure. They remain unfinished inside us.**

Perhaps this is why childhood and old age resemble one another—not because both depend on others, but because both stand at the threshold of time. One at the beginning. One at the opening toward something else.

And one more thought: the Little Prince has traveled the universe. He has lived long enough to understand loss, responsibility, and departure. By any measure, he is old. And yet he remains a child.

The view from here is simple.

Aging is the childhood of wisdom.

Exercises Chapter 2

1. The Day That Refuses to End

Choose one ordinary day from your past—not a milestone, not a trauma. A day that *should* have disappeared.

Write it as if it never ended.

- Do not summarize.
- Stay inside the day.
- Let time stretch, stall, or loop.

Avoid explanation. Let sensory detail—light, temperature, sound—carry meaning.

Prompt:
That day never ended because…

2. Letters to the Body

The body has been your longest companion. It remembers what the mind forgets. Write a letter to one part of your body (a knee, a scar, the hands, the back, the heart).

- Address it directly.
- Thank it for something it endured.
- Ask it one question.

Do not romanticize pain; acknowledge it without apology.

Constraint:
Write in the second person (“you”).

3. What I Know Now (Without Explaining It)

Wisdom loses power when it becomes advice. Write a list of 10 things you know now that you did not know at 20.

But:

- Do not explain how you learned them.
- Do not justify them.
- Do not moralize.

Each sentence should stand alone, like a fragment carved in stone.

Example starter:
I know now that waiting is a form of action.

4. The Object That Survived Me

Objects outlive phases of our lives. They are witnesses. Choose an object you have owned for decades—or one you lost long ago.

Write its biography.

- Where did it come from?
- What has it seen?
- What does it know about you that others do not?

You may write in the object's voice, or remain an observer.

Ending prompt:
If it could speak now, it would say…

5. The Conversation That Never Happened

Some conversations mature too late. That does not mean they are lost. Write a dialogue between yourself and someone you never fully spoke to:

- a parent,
- a former friend,
- a younger version of yourself,
- or someone no longer alive.

Let silence appear on the page.
Use pauses. Interruptions. Unfinished sentences.

Rule:
No reconciliation is required.

6. Today, Written Slowly

Attention deepens with age.Describe *today* as if it were the first and last day you would ever write.

- Write in the present tense.
- Avoid metaphor for the first paragraph.
- Notice what usually escapes notice.

Only in the final lines may you allow abstraction or reflection.

Closing line prompt:
This is what today gave me.

The Place of All Places

The future does not come from ahead; it grows from within us. It is not a distant promise advancing toward us on a linear track, but the slow ripening of everything we have lived, remembered, forgotten, and transformed. I once believed the future was the horizon—an ever-receding line that mocked movement. The faster I walked, the farther it seemed to retreat. Now I understand it otherwise. The future is not where we are going; it is what continues to become inside us, even—perhaps especially—as we age.

This intuition aligns with what philosopher Alan Watts once suggested when he reminded us that the universe is not a thing but an event, not an object but a happening. We are not *in* time; we are *time doing itself here*. From this perspective, the future is not an unopened room waiting down the corridor, but the ongoing modulation of presence. To live, then, is not to march forward, but to participate—again and again—in the unfolding of what already is.

Every time I write, I touch that invisible place where unfolding happens. Words, after all, are not containers; they are seeds. They do not bloom on command. They require patience, warmth, and the almost forgotten discipline of silence. Often, while drafting a paragraph, I feel I am writing for someone who does not yet exist: a reader I will never meet, a grandchild not yet born, or a future version of myself who will one day return to the page and recognize something I could not yet name. Perhaps this is why writing endures. Language continues living after we stop speaking. It does not belong to the moment of its utterance; it belongs to the place where meaning keeps arriving late.

Walt Whitman understood this intuitively. In *Leaves of Grass*, he writes:

"I tramp a perpetual journey,
(Come listen all!)
My signs are a rain-proof coat, good shoes, and a staff cut from the woods."

Whitman's journey is not toward a destination but into an expanding sense of belonging. Place, for him, is not geography but participation. He does not ask where he is going; he declares where he is—*here*, in motion, in breath, in the body's intelligence. The road is not ahead of him; it emerges beneath his feet.

This sense of place as an interior–exterior continuum finds a striking parallel in the work of Jacobo Grinberg, who proposed that reality itself is not a fixed structure but a relational field generated between perception and consciousness. For Grinberg, space is not something we occupy; it is something we co-create. What we call "the world" arises from the resonance between inner states and external patterns. In this light, the place of all places is not a point on a map, but a living interface—a threshold where inner life and outer form briefly coincide.

Writing happens precisely at that threshold. It is neither purely internal nor entirely external. It is an act of translation, a tuning between what insists from within and what the world allows to be said. When we write later in life, this tuning deepens. Experience has thinned illusion. Silence has become articulate. The page no longer demands conquest; it invites conversation.

This is why Hannah Arendt's notion of *natality* feels especially resonant here. She argued that human beings are defined not only by mortality, but by their capacity to begin. Every act of creation—however modest—is a new beginning. Writing a sentence is not the repetition of the past; it is the appearance of something that did not exist before. Aging, then, is not merely a descent into closure, but a turning: from urgency to fecundity, from ambition to resonance. To grow old is not to exhaust beginnings, but to learn how to begin again—more quietly, more precisely.

Ralph Waldo Emerson, writing in *Nature*, gestures toward this expansive understanding of place when he observes:

"I am glad to the brink of fear."

The line is deceptively simple. Emerson does not locate joy in certainty, but at the edge—where perception widens and the self loosens its grip. Place, here, is not safety but openness. It is the moment when one stands inside the world rather than above it. In later life, writing can recover this stance: not mastery, but attunement.

In old age, time loses its sharp edges. Mornings arrive more slowly, yet thoughts feel denser, more luminous. The imagination does not disappear; it refines itself. There is less need to invent worlds because the world, at last, begins to speak back. What once required effort now requires listening. This is the writer's task at this stage of life: to harvest what time has already planted, to write from abundance rather than lack.

Mary Oliver once wrote that *attention is the beginning of devotion*. Writing, for us, becomes precisely this form of attention. A way of saying to life: *I am still here. I am still listening.* Each story, poem, or fragment extends our breath into tomorrow. Not as a claim to immortality, but as a gesture of continuation—a sentence that refuses to end because life itself has not finished speaking.

So if you ask me now what the future is, I will answer without looking ahead. The future is the next page waiting to be written. It is the word trembling before it finds its place. It is the quiet courage to begin once more—not because we believe everything is still possible, but because we know that something always is.

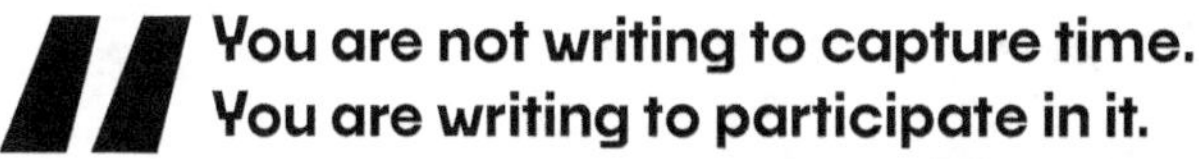

**You are not writing to capture time.
You are writing to participate in it.**

**The place of all places is not elsewhere.
It is the page — where what you have lived continues to become.**

The place of all places is not behind us or before us. It is here—where memory, perception, and language briefly meet. And from that meeting, the future continues to grow.

Exercises Chapter 3

1. The Inner Geography Map

Place is not where you are, but how you inhabit. Write a map of your inner geography.

- Divide the page into sections with titles such as *Threshold*, *Desert*, *Garden*, *Room with No Windows*, *Open Road*.
- For each section, write a short paragraph describing what lives there now.
- Do not explain what these places “mean.” Let them remain experiential.

Guiding question:
Where do I spend most of my inner time these days?

2. The Sentence That Keeps Becoming

The future grows from within language itself. Begin with a single sentence you believe is finished. Then rewrite it six times, each time allowing it to open differently.

- Change rhythm, not meaning.
- Let the sentence age with you.
- The final version should feel less resolved, more alive.

Constraint:
Do not delete the sentence—only transform it.

3. Writing from the Threshold

Writing happens between inner and outer worlds.Sit near a physical threshold: a doorway, window, balcony, porch, or hallway. Write for 15 minutes, alternating sentences:

- One sentence describing what you see or hear.
- One sentence describing what stirs internally.

Let the boundary blur.

Closing line:
Here is where the two meet.

4. The Unwritten Reader

Writing is addressed to someone who may not yet exist. Write a short piece addressed to a reader who is not alive yet—or not yet ready to read you.

This reader could be:

- A grandchild
- A future self
- A stranger decades from now

Do not instruct. Do not advise. Simply speak.

Opening line:
By the time you read this…

5. The Place That Writes You Back

Place is relational, not static. Choose a place that has accompanied you for many years (a house, street, town, landscape).

Write in two voices:

- Your voice, describing the place
- The place's voice, responding to you

Let the place remember things you forgot.

Rule:
The place must disagree with you at least once.

6. Beginning Again, Differently

Aging as renewed natality. Write about a beginning that did *not* feel like one at the time:

- ☐ A quiet decision
- ☐ A small loss
- ☐ A shift in attention
- ☐ A slowing down

Write it as a beginning now.

Final line (required):
This is where it began, though I didn't know it then.

The Body Remembers

I have always thought of memory as something that happens inside the mind, a kind of private cinema flickering behind the eyes. Memory, I thought, was a merely an archive: selective, narrative, obedient to language. But with age, a new quieter and more unsettling thought has overcome me: memory lives elsewhere. It lives in the knees that ache before the rain arrives, in the scar that tightens without warning, in the hands that tremble not from fear but from decades of use. The body remembers everything the mind politely forgets.

The body is our oldest book. Long before we learned to read or write, it was already recording. It carries marginal notes from every chapter of our life: the small burn on a finger from a stove no one recalls touching, the deep grooves in the shoulders where work once pressed its invisible weight, the altered rhythm of breathing that announces grief before the mind dares to name it. The body does not summarize; it retains. Its memory is not chronological but accumulative, layered, dense. Where the mind edits, the body archives.

Walt Whitman intuited this with remarkable clarity when he wrote, *"I sing the body electric."* For Whitman, the body is not a vessel that carries experience; it *is* experience itself—charged, permeable, inseparable from meaning. Long after youth fades, this insight remains radical. The body is not the past we outgrow; it is the past that continues speaking in us, even when we no longer know how to translate it.

This understanding finds a deep resonance in the poetry of Rumi, who never treated the body as a prison to be escaped, but as a threshold to be crossed again and again. Rumi often describes the body as a house—not the self, but the place where life arrives. *"This body is a guesthouse,"* he writes, *"every morning a new arrival."* Joy, sorrow, fatigue, illness, longing: all enter through the body first. The task is not to deny these guests, but to receive them. Forgetting this hospitality is what leads us astray—not embodiment itself.

In teaching creative writing to elders, I often tell my students that the page begins under the skin. Stories do not arrive fully formed from inspiration; they rise from sensation. The faint ringing in the ear at night, the smell of rain on metal, the peculiar heaviness of sleep after loss—these are not distractions from writing. They are its raw materials. Language does not invent meaning; it translates what the body already knows but cannot articulate on its own.

Rumi understood this pedagogy of sensation through pain. *"Where there is ruin, there is hope for a treasure,"* he writes. The "ruin" is often bodily: illness, fatigue, the slow betrayal of strength. These experiences fracture the illusion of mastery. They teach us not by adding knowledge, but by removing certainty. The body instructs precisely where it weakens. A scar does not explain itself; it insists. A tremor does not justify its presence; it speaks anyway.

Old age, in this sense, becomes a profound act of translation. The body speaks more slowly now, often in fragments, pauses, and repetitions. Yet its meanings deepen. There is humility in learning to inhabit a form that softens, weakens, loosens. This is not a failure of design. It is the body returning to its elemental grammar: the curve instead of the line, the breath instead of the command, the pause instead of the acceleration. Rumi likened the body to a lute and the soul to its musician. A lute is not discarded when its strings slacken; it is retuned. The music changes, but it does not end.

This retuning alters how memory functions. The mind prefers coherence, causality, explanation. The body resists all three. It remembers without narrative. It remembers without forgiveness or resentment. It remembers in sensation, posture, reflex. Writing from the body means accepting this opacity—allowing sensation to lead without demanding resolution. The page becomes less a mirror of thought than an extension of listening.

I think again of my grandmother. When she could no longer walk long distances, she said, almost casually, "The world comes to me now." At the time, I heard resignation. What I hear now is wisdom. When motion slows, perception widens. When the body travels less, attention travels more. Rumi would have recognized this immediately. He urged us not to resist the changes that come our way, but to *let life live through us*. The aging body, less defended and less distracted, becomes porous. Wind enters. Memory enters. Silence enters.

This porosity transforms writing. Earlier in life, writing often feels like an act of will: pushing through, producing, proving. Later, it becomes an act of reception. The question is no longer *What can I make happen?* but *What is asking to be heard?* The body, patient and exacting, becomes the primary informant. Writing is no longer extracted from experience; it is distilled from it.

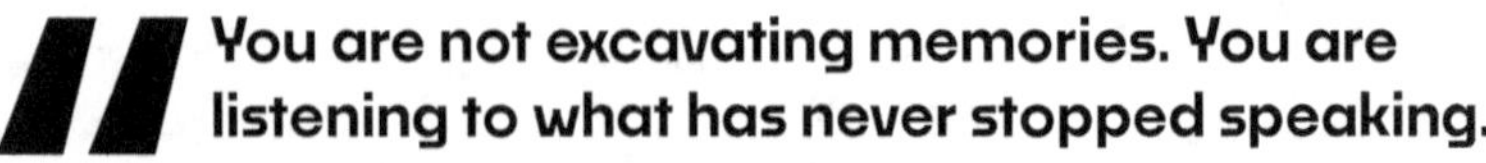

You are not excavating memories. You are listening to what has never stopped speaking.

The body does not remember to explain. It remembers to endure.

Ralph Waldo Emerson once observed that *"the creation of a thousand forests is in one acorn."* The body is that acorn. It contains more than we can see. A lifetime of gestures, labors, loves, injuries, and recoveries resides in its smallest movements. When we write later in life, we are not impoverished by time; we are saturated with it. The difficulty is not remembering more, but trusting what has already been remembered for us.

When I sit down to write now, I notice the weight of my hands resting on the keyboard. I notice the pulse beneath the wrist, steady and unremarkable, insisting nonetheless. It reminds me that the story I am writing is also being written *through* me. The body participates. It corrects tone. It slows the sentence. It interrupts when truth arrives too quickly.

Rumi warned against cleverness divorced from embodiment. *"Sell your cleverness and buy bewilderment,"* he wrote, because bewilderment is the condition in which the body regains authority. Aging ushers us naturally into this state—not confusion, but openness. Less armored. Less certain. More available.

Perhaps this is the final lesson aging offers the writer: memory is not something we retrieve. It is something we inhabit. The body has been holding the record all along—patient, exacting, unsentimental. The body writes first, always. Words follow as echoes—necessary, imperfect, human.

Exercises Chapter 4

1. The Scar That Speaks

The body remembers without explaining. Choose one physical mark—visible or invisible: a scar, ache, stiffness, tremor, or recurring sensation.

Write from the perspective of that mark.

- Do not explain how it happened.
- Do not narrate its origin.
- Let it speak only of what it *knows*, not what it *means*.

Constraint:
The word *"I"* may only appear if it belongs to the body part, not to you.

Closing line:
This is what I carry.

2. Memory Without Story

The body remembers without narrative or causality. Write a page composed only of bodily sensations linked to a single period of your life (childhood, working years, grief, illness, love).

- No names.
- No dates.
- No explanations.

Use fragments. Let repetition occur. Allow gaps.

Guiding question:
What does the body recall when the mind stays silent?

3. The Guesthouse Inventory

The body as a house of arrivals (after Rumi). Write a list of “guests” that currently visit your body.

These may include:

- ▯ Fatigue
- ▯ Warmth
- ▯ Anxiety
- ▯ Stillness
- ▯ Pain
- ▯ Calm
- ▯ Hunger
- ▯ Lightness

For each guest, write 2–3 sentences describing how it enters, where it stays, and how long it remains.

Rule:
No guest may be judged as good or bad.

4. Writing From the Pause

Aging slows the body, deepens meaning. Set a timer for 10 minutes.

Write only during moments when you *pause*:

- Pause between sentences.
- Pause between breaths.
- Pause when you feel unsure.

Let the pauses shape the text. White space is part of the writing.

Prompt:
I stop here because…

5. The Sentence the Body Interrupts

The body corrects language. Begin writing a confident, articulate paragraph about a memory.

When you notice a bodily response (tightness, emotion, fatigue, breath change), stop immediately.

Then rewrite the paragraph *from that sensation*, not from thought.

Reflection question:
What did the body refuse to let me say?

6. Bewilderment as Wisdom

Letting go of cleverness; trusting embodied knowing. Write about something you no longer fully understand—but once believed you did.

Do not seek resolution.

Let uncertainty remain active, alive, unfinished.

Required final line:
I do not know this anymore, and that is how it stays with me.

What Remains

Grief does not arrive all at once. It does not knock. It seeps. It enters through the body before the mind has found a name for it. A heaviness in the chest that appears without warning. A fatigue that has no clear cause. A pause in the middle of an ordinary gesture. Only later do we understand: something is missing. Someone is no longer where they used to be.

Emily Dickinson understood this wordless arrival when she wrote that pain has "*an element of blank*." Grief begins in that blankness—before interpretation, before narrative, before consolation. It announces itself not through thought but through interruption. Something falters. Something hesitates. The body knows before the mind is ready to agree.

For a long time, I believed grief was an emotion—intense, disruptive, temporary. Something to be endured and then, eventually, overcome. Age has taught me otherwise. Grief is not an emotion. It is a condition. A way the world rearranges itself after a bond has been broken. It is memory that has lost its destination.

C. S. Lewis, writing after the death of his wife, observed with stark clarity: *"No one ever told me that grief felt so like fear."* What he named was not panic, but disorientation—the sense that the ground itself has shifted. Grief alters the architecture of the world. The rooms are the same, but their proportions feel wrong. Doors open where walls once stood. Familiar paths no longer lead where we expect.

The body knows this first. Long before the mind articulates loss, the body registers absence. It reaches for what is no longer there. It wakes at the wrong hour. It forgets the weight it has learned to carry and then remembers again. Grief settles into posture, into breath, into the small hesitations that interrupt our days. It is not loud. It is persistent.

When someone we love dies—or leaves irrevocably—the body continues the relationship without consent. It keeps listening for a voice that will not return. It remembers routines that no longer have a place to land. This is why grief feels so disorienting: the world remains visible, functional, intact, but our orientation within it has shifted. We are standing in the same room, yet nothing is in its proper place.

Rainer Maria Rilke once wrote that *"the future enters into us, in order to transform itself in us, long before it happens."* Grief works in the opposite direction. The past enters us and refuses to leave. It transforms the present not by appearing, but by withdrawing. What is absent becomes active. What is gone becomes formative.

In this sense, grief is the most honest form of memory. It does not allow us to curate the past or arrange it into narrative coherence. It resists closure. It refuses the logic of "moving on." Grief insists on duration. It stays.

For those of us who have lived long enough to accumulate losses, grief does not come singly. It layers. It folds. One absence awakens another. The death of a friend recalls a parent. The illness of a partner resurrects an earlier fear. Grief is cumulative, not because we are weak, but because we are faithful. We remember because we loved.

There is a particular kind of grief that belongs to old age—not sharper, but deeper. It is the grief of repetition. The grief of knowing the pattern. The grief of recognizing, too quickly, the familiar signs: the quiet before the phone rings, the careful tone of a voice, the body's sudden certainty before the words arrive. This knowledge does not protect us. It only shortens the distance between what we fear and what becomes real.

W. H. Auden captured this unbearable recognition when he wrote, *"The words of a dead man are modified in the guts of the living."* Grief is precisely this modification. The dead do not leave us unchanged. They are metabolized. They alter our inner chemistry. Their absence works on us continuously, reshaping how we speak, how we listen, how we endure.

And yet, grief is not only about death. It also attends the slow losses that aging brings: the loss of strength, of speed, of roles once inhabited without thought. We grieve capacities even as we adapt to their absence. We grieve futures that will no longer unfold as imagined. We grieve versions of ourselves that recede quietly, without ceremony.

These losses rarely receive acknowledgment. There are no rituals for the end of a certain kind of walking, a certain way of working, a certain intensity of desire. But the body marks them nonetheless. Grief does not require permission to exist. It takes up residence wherever attachment once lived.

Writing, at this stage of life, cannot avoid grief—and should not try to. To write honestly is to allow grief its full complexity: not as a problem to be solved, but as a presence to be carried. The page becomes a place where grief can speak without being corrected. Where it does not need to make sense. Where it can remain unfinished.

This is not the same as confession. Grief does not always want to be told as story. Often, it resists narrative altogether. It prefers fragments. Images. Repetition. Silence. Writing that honors grief learns to slow down, to leave space, to tolerate incompletion. It learns that what cannot be resolved can still be expressed.

There is a temptation, especially in later life, to tidy grief—to turn it into wisdom too quickly, to redeem it with meaning. But grief does not ask to be redeemed. It asks to be acknowledged. It asks to be allowed its weight. To rush past it is not strength; it is avoidance.

At the same time, grief is not sterile. It is generative in unexpected ways. It sharpens attention. It alters scale. After loss, what once seemed urgent loses its claim. What remains is often smaller, quieter, more precise. Grief teaches us what matters by stripping away what does not.

This stripping is painful, but it is also clarifying. Grief reveals the depth of our bonds. It reminds us that we have lived in relation, not isolation. In this way, grief prepares us—slowly, reluctantly—for a shift in perspective. The self, once imagined as singular, begins to loosen. We start to sense that our life has always been braided with others, that our story cannot be told alone.

Grief is where the first person begins to fracture.
Not into nothingness,
but into plurality.

After loss, we often speak differently. More carefully. More sparsely. Words acquire weight. Silence acquires dignity. Writing becomes less about expression and more about listening—to what remains, to what continues, to what asks for care. Grief reorients language away from display and toward presence.

This is why grief belongs where it does in this book—after the body has taught us to remember, and before we learn to speak in the plural. Grief is the passage between memory and belonging. It is where we discover that what we carry cannot be carried alone.

I think again of my grandmother, not only in her slowing body, but in her quiet after certain names were spoken. There were people she did not mention often, but whose absence shaped her days. Grief had settled into her movements, her pauses, her way of listening. It did not disappear. It matured. It became part of how she inhabited the world.

This is what grief does when it is allowed to stay. It does not dominate; it integrates. It becomes a lens through which we see more carefully, love more deliberately, speak more honestly. It does not erase joy, but it changes its texture. Joy becomes gentler, less possessive, more grateful.

For writers in old age, grief is not an obstacle to creativity. It is one of its deepest sources. Not because suffering produces art, but because grief clarifies attachment. It reminds us what mattered enough to leave a mark. Writing from grief is writing from fidelity.

Grief does not ask to be solved.
It asks to be listened to — slowly,
patiently, without correction.

These exercises are not meant to
complete grief,
but to give it a place to speak.

And fidelity, ultimately, is what carries us toward the next chapter. Grief does not end in isolation. It opens us—slowly, unwillingly—toward others. Toward shared memory. Toward the understanding that our losses are never only ours. That the people we grieve live on not only in us, but in the networks of care, language, and story that surround us.

Grief teaches us how to carry what cannot be restored.
And in doing so, it prepares us for a different way of speaking—
one that no longer insists on *I*,
but begins, quietly, to say *we*.

What remains when someone is gone is not emptiness.
It is relation, altered but enduring.
It is the weight that teaches us how to hold one another.

And from that weight,
another kind of book begins to open.

Exercises Chapter 5

1. The Absence That Has Weight

Explore grief as a physical presence rather than a story. Write about something that is no longer present, but still has weight in your body.

- Do not name the person, object, or loss.
- Describe only how the absence is felt physically: posture, breath, movement, fatigue.

Constraint:
No metaphors. Stay literal.

Closing line:
This is how it remains.

2. Writing the Disorientation

To honor grief as a rearrangement of reality. Describe a familiar place (a room, a street, a kitchen) *after* a loss.

- The place must remain unchanged.
- Only your orientation to it has shifted.

Focus on what feels “off,” disproportionate, or misaligned.

Guiding question:
What no longer fits where it once did?

3. The Sentence That Will Not Finish

To work with grief against resistance to closure. Begin a sentence about loss and allow it to remain unfinished.

- Write three versions of the same sentence.
- Let each version trail off in a different way.

Do not complete the thought.

Example opening:
Since you left, I keep noticing…

4. Layered Loss

To acknowledge cumulative grief. Write three short paragraphs, each about a different loss from different periods of your life.

- Do not compare them.
- Do not explain connections.

Let the echoes emerge on their own.

Final instruction:
Read the three paragraphs aloud, slowly.

5. Speaking Differently

To observe how grief alters language. Rewrite a short piece of writing you produced earlier in your life (a letter, journal entry, or memory).

Then rewrite it again *as you would now*, after grief.

Notice:

- what has slowed,
- what has disappeared,
- what has gained weight.

Reflection prompt:
What does my voice carry now that it didn't before?

6. From I to We

To prepare the transition toward shared memory and belonging. Write about a loss using “I.”

Then rewrite the same piece using “we.”

- The “we” may include the living, the dead, the remembered, or the unnamed.
- Do not clarify who belongs to it.

Final line (required):
This could not be carried alone.

Thinking in Constellations

Every life is a page in a larger book, written in many hands, across generations. When we write, we are never alone at the desk. The sentences we form carry the syntax of those who spoke before us—their cadences, gestures, hesitations, their ways of naming what could not be fully said. Even the blank spaces between our words belong to someone: a mother's pause before difficult news, a friend's absence that reshaped a conversation, a teacher's unfinished thought that continues working inside us long after the class has ended.

In youth, we imagine our stories as singular, unrepeatable, sealed by the authority of the first person. We say *I* with conviction, believing that authorship means origin. But as time thickens, another awareness emerges: our words echo. We begin to hear that what we call "our voice" is braided from many voices, and that our most intimate sentences are already communal.

This dawning recognition is what I call ***Thinking in Constellations***—the invisible archive of being together, written without a single author, revised endlessly by living and dying.

Walt Whitman sensed this expansiveness when he declared, *"I am large, I contain multitudes."* The line is often quoted, but its ethical force is sometimes overlooked. Whitman was not celebrating ego; he was dissolving it. To contain multitudes is to admit that the self is porous, that identity is composed rather than owned. Writing, in this sense, is not an act of self-expression but of self-recognition: we discover who we are by encountering who has already spoken through us.

When I think about memory now, I no longer imagine it as mine. The stories I tell belong to the people who made them possible: my grandmother climbing that mountain with a determination I inherited without realizing it; my mother bringing books home, teaching us—without instruction—that language is a form of shelter; my students, who remind me daily that writing is not a luxury but a mode of survival. To write about oneself is always to write about everyone who entered the sentence, even briefly, even silently.

This idea resonates deeply with the spiritual teachings of Rumi, who insisted that the self is never solitary. *"Why are you so busy with this or that or good or bad,"* he asks, *"pay attention to how things blend."* For Rumi, blending is not confusion; it is truth. Lives interpenetrate. Meanings arise in relation. The soul itself, he suggests, is not a private possession but a crossing point—a place where many currents meet. In this light, Thinking in Constellations is not metaphorical. It is the actual condition of existence.

Time, too, changes its meaning here. It ceases to behave like a straight line stretching from birth to death and begins to feel circular, communal, shared. What I remember is no longer important only because it happened to me, but because it may be needed by someone else—now or later. Memory becomes a form of transmission. Forgetting, too, acquires dignity. What I let go of may be precisely what allows others to breathe, to speak, to begin. Even erasure has purpose: it clears space on the page.

The philosopher Walter Benjamin once suggested that every generation is endowed with a "weak messianic power"—not the power to redeem the world all at once, but the responsibility to pass something on. Writing participates in that responsibility. It does not rescue the past; it keeps it legible. Each story is a hand extended forward, not to claim authority, but to offer continuity.

Old age, then, is not an ending. It is a passage into plurality. Gradually, often without ceremony, we move from *I* to *we*: the collective pronoun of experience. This shift is not a loss of identity but its expansion. To write in that plural is to acknowledge that language itself is communal, that every word we use was once borrowed, inhabited, worn down by use, and passed on. No word belongs to us alone. We inherit language the way we inherit breath.

This is why writing, later in life, begins to resemble a ceremony rather than a performance. It is no longer about originality in the narrow sense, but about alignment—placing one's voice carefully within a long, ongoing conversation. The page becomes a gathering place. To write is to say: *I was here, and I was not alone.*

I often imagine a future reader—someone young, restless, searching—opening a book and finding in it the faint trace of our time: our hesitations, our tenderness, our attempts to make sense of what it meant to be human under these particular skies. They may not know our names. They may not remember the dates. But they will feel something between the lines: a warmth, a steadiness, the sense that others have stood where they now stand. That, perhaps, is legacy—not fame or permanence, but continuity of care. A sentence that makes room. A story that says, *you are not the first, and you will not be the last.*

You are not writing to claim a voice.
You are writing to join one.

Every page is already crowded.
And that is its beauty.

And so, dear reader, this is not my book. It is ours. Each story you have written while reading, each memory you have touched or released, becomes another page in **Thinking in Constellations**. One day, someone else will write in its margins, adding their handwriting beside ours. They will revise what we began. They will misunderstand us in productive ways. They will continue the sentence.

Perhaps that is what eternity truly is:
not an afterlife,
but an afterword.

Exercises Chapter 6

1. The Sentence I Did Not Write Alone

Write one sentence that feels unmistakably yours. Then write a second paragraph tracing where that sentence came from.

- Whose voice echoes in it?
- Whose rhythm, silence, or hesitation shaped it?

You may name people—or leave them unnamed.

Closing line:
This sentence carries more than me.

2. Writing in the Plural

Moving from *I* to *we*. Rewrite a personal memory entirely using **"we"** instead of "I."

- Let the "we" remain ambiguous.
- It may include the living, the dead, the absent, the imagined.

Notice how meaning shifts.

Reflection question:
Who enters the story when I stop writing alone?

3. Marginal Notes

The invisible authors of our lives. Choose a moment from your past. Write it briefly.

Then write the same moment as if it were a **marginal note** in someone else's book.

- ▯ Short.
- ▯ Observant.
- ▯ Slightly unfinished.

Constraint:
Do not explain the event—only annotate it.

4. The Story I Carry for Someone Else

Memory as transmission.Write a story you believe someone else will need someday.

Do not identify who they are.

Write with care, not instruction.

Opening line:
I am leaving this here in case you need it.

5. Borrowed Words

Language as communal material. List five words or phrases you often use.

For each, write:

- Who you learned it from (or might have).
- What part of your life it belongs to.

Then write a short paragraph using all five words, acknowledging their borrowed life.

6. The Afterword

Write as continuity, not closure.Imagine someone reading your work many years after you are gone.

Write the **afterword they might add**.

- Let it misunderstand you slightly.
- Let it continue rather than conclude.

Final line (required):
This is how the sentence went on.

.

Coda: The Last Hand on the Page

There are sentences that do not belong to narrative, that resist being placed inside a sequence. They arrive as interruptions—events that fracture continuity rather than extend it. Like saying, “I had open-heart surgery.” This is one of them.

I was afraid. Not abstractly, not philosophically, but with the precision of the body recognizing its own limit. Fear, in that moment, was not an emotion but a form of knowledge: the sudden clarity that the story could end here, without completion, without revision.

And yet, it did not.

I remained.

Again, I remained.

It is difficult to speak, without distortion, of the number of times life has approached that threshold—the point at which the possible narrows into a single, irreversible outcome. At twenty-three. At twenty-seven. At thirty-five. And others, less easily numbered, less willing to be named.

One begins to understand, not through reflection but through recurrence, that survival is not an achievement. It is a condition one inhabits provisionally.

Perhaps this is why I have always trusted animals more than explanations. A cat does not anticipate its end; it occupies its present with an intensity that does not require justification. It lives within the field of the possible without converting that field into anxiety. It does not narrate what might happen. It remains.

The human difficulty lies precisely there: we know that what is possible may occur.

Possibility is not benign. It is symmetrical. It opens in both directions. If something can happen, it can happen.

This is not pessimism. It is structure.

We move within that structure, making choices that feel decisive, though they are never final. We choose paths, but we do not choose the conditions under which those paths unfold. There is, always, a remainder—a margin where contingency operates without our consent.

Until, eventually, the structure closes.

We read the gestures, the silences, the partial sentences that others leave behind, often without knowing they have written them. No life arrives untouched. No voice begins at its own origin. We inherit language already marked—phrases worn by repetition, words shaped by prior breath, pauses refined by generations of use.

We enter that language not as owners, but as participants.

We adjust it—sometimes with care, sometimes with imprecision—and then we pass it forward, altered by our passage through it.

What we call time—past, present, future—does not divide experience as cleanly as grammar suggests. These are not separate territories but overlapping attentions. The past persists as relevance. The future appears as projection. The present is not a point but a convergence.

What matters is not when something occurred, but how it continues.

To arrive at a moment in which one can shed the surface of identity while language remains intact—this is not transcendence. It is recognition. The recognition that meaning was never contained within the self.

Nothing we have lived belongs exclusively to us.

Not memory. Not grief. Not love. Not fear.

Each arrives already structured, already named in advance by voices that preceded us, and each will be reconfigured again by those who receive it after us.

Writing does not interrupt this movement. It reveals it.

It allows us to see that what we thought was singular was always relational. The task, then, is not longevity. It is calibration.

To grow older is inevitable. To grow better requires attention.

Better is not perfection. It is openness. It is the refusal to close the sentence prematurely, to declare meaning where only process exists.

As long as possibility remains active, the text is not finished.

And as long as the text is not finished. Neither are we.

Age, if it offers any authority, does not do so through certainty. It offers discernment: the capacity to recognize what need not be resolved, what must be released, what can be entrusted to others without guarantee of return.

The older writer does not conclude. They delimit.

They do not seal the text. They create passages.

At this point, the page no longer appears as a surface upon which one inscribes experience. It becomes a site—a shared terrain where multiple lives intersect without requiring coherence.

The page is not paper. It is the condition of relation.

It carries both density and openness: the accumulation of what has been lived and the exposure to what has not yet found articulation.

To write, here, is not to produce.

It is to move.

Writing becomes a form of walking—measured, attentive, receptive to irregularities in the ground. One advances without claiming mastery over the terrain.

There is, in this movement, an ethical reorientation.

Earlier, writing seeks affirmation: evidence that one has existed, that one has left a trace capable of being recognized.

Later, writing seeks transmission.

The question shifts. Not: Will I be remembered? But: What can remain in use? Not: What is my story? But: What continues through it? The self does not disappear. It recalibrates. It occupies less space, but with greater precision.

Memory, then, discloses its function.

It is not storage.

It is circulation.

What we remember is not what we preserve intact, but what we allow to move through others. What we forget is not necessarily loss. It is clearance—a necessary opening that prevents language from solidifying into monument.

For language that hardens ceases to serve. It becomes inert.

In this sense, later life does not contract experience. It expands its address. One no longer writes from the self as origin, but through the self as medium. The body, the past, the accumulated voices—none of these are endpoints. They are conduits.The "I" loosens. And in that loosening, something more stable appears: a steadiness of attention, a discipline of care, a capacity to speak without insisting on finality.

This book has returned, repeatedly, to a single insistence: writing is not an accomplishment.

It is a practice.

A practice that binds memory to embodiment, solitude to relation, presence to continuation.

Its exercises were never tasks. They were thresholds They remain open. They ask of the writer what time itself asks: patience, clarity, and the courage to remain incomplete. Writing and aging converge precisely here. Both reduce velocity. Both displace certainty. Both require listening where one once demanded control. What remains, when urgency recedes, is attention.

And attention—when sustained without demand—becomes a form of care.

Not the care that rescues or resolves, but the care that accompanies.

The care that remains with what cannot be repaired, that returns to what resists simplification, that holds space for what has not yet entered language.

This is the form of attention that endures. It is not expressive. It is exact. It does not seek to preserve everything. It knows, with precision, what cannot be retained. And still, it tends. Whoever encounters these pages will not encounter a person. They will encounter a posture.

A way of inhabiting time without exhausting it. They may not name it, but they will recognize its orientation: an effort to listen without closing, to speak without final claim, to leave the text permeable.If anything remains, it will not be the voice. It will be the gesture.

So this coda does not conclude. It pauses.

We leave the page open.

www.ingramcontent.com/pod-product-compliance
Lightning Source LLC
LaVergne TN
LVHW010620100826
845148LV00014B/3045

* 9 7 9 8 9 0 4 5 2 9 4 7 5 *